1

The Letter to Dad

A Conversion Story

by

Andrew Emmans

3

Anselm Viator Publishing

2124 W Wild Rose Rd

Colbert, WA 99005

2023

ISBN 978-1-387-28893-9

Imprint: Lulu.com

<u>Contents</u>

"See ye that I have not labored for myself only, but for all that seek out the truth."

Ecclesiasticus 24:47

Preface

The following is a personal letter, originally written to my father, and it relates the story of my conversion from the Protestant religion to the Catholic Church. It is a story that will be familiar to most Catholics, I think, in some form or another; for it merely describes the wayfaring course of one soul, responding to what Saint Thomas Aquinas calls, "*the inward instinct of the Divine invitation.*" It is the timeless tale of man's journey *from* God, *back to* God; timeless because it is a story as old as time. It is simply the story of sin, redemption, and the mercy of God, played out in the unfolding drama of one human life. We all make this journey back to God, if we are men of good will; indeed, we *must* make it, no matter the cost, because this is the only path that can ever lead to happiness. It is the only road home. The story is unique only insofar as its author, the protagonist of the journey, is unique; unique in identity, and in circumstance; a man made in the image and likeness of God, for whom our Blessed Lord spent His precious blood to the last drop; "*Greater love hath no man than this, that he lay down his life for his friend.*"

If this story is a familiar one, I hope that it will at least be a consolation to whomsoever might happen to take up and read. We sometimes find it very helpful to hear the personal stories of others who have walked a treacherous path, seeking the narrow gate; as our Lord has said: "*Strive to enter by the narrow gate; for many, I say to you, shall seek to enter, and shall not be able.*" If we all must make the journey through the narrow gate, we still sometimes grow weary on the way. To read of the perils through which God has brought others can be a great comfort. I hope and pray that this little work is at least that to some other wayfarer. For although the way is narrow, and although we must strive, carrying our own crosses, yet our Lord is so merciful. He gives grace; He lightens the load.

Nor has the story yet ended for this *viator*, this wayfarer. After escaping the web of errors that is the Protestant religion, I jumped feet first into the fire of the *Novus Ordo* church. That Catholicism is true I judged rightly; I erred in practice, however, by mistaking the "conciliar church," the *Novus Ordo* religion, the Vatican II sect, for the Catholic Church. We live in very strange times. Perhaps the reader does not know it, but we are in the middle of what Sacred Scripture calls the *great apostasy*; the great falling away. Further, the Catholic Church suffers today under the grievous chastisement of *sedevacante*. That is to say, we have no living head, no supernatural principle of unity: we have no Pope. We have had none, apparently, since the death of Pope Pius XII in 1958. Difficult and strange words, no doubt. But the realization is also consoling; it explains the moral and religious chaos coming from the Vatican, and from the clergy of the new religion, who are merely aping Catholic clergy; it also explains the ceaseless blasphemy and wickedness in high places, from the very men claiming to be the Vicars of our Blessed Lord and Savior Jesus Christ. The Vatican II, *Novus Ordo* religion is an impostor religion, complete with imposter sacraments, imposter priests and Bishops, and imposter Cardinals and Popes; and it has entrenched itself, like a cancer, in the hallowed halls of Catholicism. Seek though you will, you cannot find the Catholic Church in her former churches, Basilicas and Cathedrals, however magnificent; it has been driven into the wilderness.

I did not know this when I fled from the Protestant religion at the age of twenty-six; the journey back to God is a perilous endeavor indeed. How true our Lord's words, that we must *strive* to enter by the narrow way! For ten years I foolishly sojourned in the *Novus Ordo* desert, with my family, until God mercifully woke me up again. It was touch and go, and but for the intervention of God, we might not have made it out. And the intervention of God came through a very particular channel: the intercession of the Blessed Virgin Mary, the Mother of God, and our Mother. She it was who became for the Emmans family the true Pole Star, the true Star of the Sea: *Stella Maris*. We would have been made irrevocably shipwreck a thousand times over but for her. She is the Hammer of Heretics, and she crushes under heal the grotesque distortions of the *Novus Ordo* religion, just as she broke in pieces the impious teachings of the Reformers, five hundred years ago. It was her Rosary that became for us a lifeline to the true faith, and to the true sacraments, and it is into her hands that we have since committed our family; she will bring the wayfaring Emmans family finally through this vale of tears, and safely home.

This short book tells half the story. There is a second part. In 2017 I delivered a talk at the annual Fatima Conference, held at the traditional Catholic parish of Mount St. Michael, in Spokane, WA. The first half of the lecture was essentially a modified form of the letter I wrote to my father in 2016, the full text of which you hold in your hand. The second half described the journey from the *Novus Ordo* sect into the traditional, Roman Catholic Church. If the reader wishes to learn more about the second stage of our journey, I have taken the liberty of including a link to my talk at the end of this book. The website which hosts the lecture has innumerable resources, and is a perfect place for those interested to begin examining the *sedevacantist* question.

I must forewarn the reader also: many of the perils described here are *moral*. In this letter I have, as it were, bared my soul. There are matters mentioned that I would sooner forget, than to publish them for the world to know. They are memories of great shame for me personally. Although unworthy to be compared to them, except in malice of former sin, I take as models for this confession the great Saint Peter, Saint Paul, and Saint Augustine. Like them, I have been forgiven much; please God, give me the grace to love much. Whatever the case, God alone is responsible for any good that I may have done, and for any success that I may have had in life; my sins are my own.

I must also emphasize the following: this letter has been published strictly under obedience. My mother requested it. There is something profoundly off-putting about publishing what amounts to one hundred pages of talking about oneself. I excuse myself with G.K. Chesterton's words, in the preface to his Orthodoxy: "*It is unavoidably affirmative and therefore unavoidably autobiographical. The writer has been driven back upon somewhat the same difficulty as that which beset Newman in writing his Apologia; he has been forced to be egotistical only in order to be sincere.*" Although egotistical, still I am not so egotistical that I consider what I have written to be worthy to loose the latchet of either Mr. Chesterton's or Cardinal Newman's autobiographical sandal, so to speak. Nevertheless, God commands obedience, and can make use of the most unworthy of instruments, if they but obey. Also, if Chesterton had a personal challenge to motivate his wonderful *apologia*, I have something greater: the first commandment with a promise.

If this letter consists of my own egotistical ramblings, the story itself is not only my own. My beautiful and longsuffering wife Jamiey is the glue that holds the tale together. No, let us state it more strongly still: it is her love that holds our family together, and has held *me* together all these long years. Many women would not have endured what she has suffered for the faith, and for her family. Her love for me, for our children, and for God, is more true and noble than I can here express. Twice in my life I have had to tell my wife that we were, in fact, in a false religion; twice she believed me, and followed me, at great personal cost, across the country and around the world.

Further, it would be another book in itself if I tried to include all the other remarkable ways in which God's providence has worked in the Emmans family. It would be too great a task to attempt to relate the incredible story of my mother's journey to the one true faith, and through the narrow gate. Or to communicate that of my brothers, Jordan, Nathan, and Peter. Or of my baby sister Lydia and her remarkable pilgrimage: how she was tried in the fire, and found worthy. My siblings and their amazing families have stories worth telling, and if they are not told here in this life, please God, they will be in the next.

Sometime during the winter of 2015-2016, when our family was in something of a turmoil over the question of the *sedevacantist* conclusion, and the traditional Catholic faith, I had a conversation with my mother. It convinced me that I had not been very clear when explaining to my father why I had converted to the Catholic faith to begin with, a decade before. My dad had remained behind, in the Protestant religion, and remains behind still. Indeed, he is very hostile to the faith to this day; and this probably because of my own poor example as a Catholic man, and my own inability to state the Catholic faith with clarity. Jamiey told me that I should just write a letter to him, to clear up all misunderstanding. On her recommendation I wrote what follows, and sent it to my dad, my mother, and my siblings. It has since been sent to other friends and family members as well. It is a meandering, reflective account of my life in relation to the true faith. It obviously involves persons and places which will mean nothing to the reader, so I have removed the last names of all non-public persons, to protect both the innocent, and the guilty. Where I thought necessary and helpful, I have added footnotes. It has been very lightly edited; although there is much that I would add or amplify, I have otherwise chosen to leave it almost exactly as I first wrote it, for better or worse. *Quod scripsi, scripsi.*

In Christ and His Blessed Mother,

Drew Emmans

Colbert, Washington
December 24th
The Vigil of the Nativity, *Anno Domini* 2022

"You believe that God is one? You do well. The demons also believe, and tremble."

James 2:19

Introduction, and the Dave Hunt Book

Dear Dad,

I very much appreciated our talk the other evening. Thank you again.

Concerning Dave Hunt, I think that it would be wise to put him on the shelf for good.[1] You mentioned that I might not appreciate his "tone." I actually do appreciate a passionate tone, especially for topics upon which hang the salvation of souls. What I don't appreciate is a public liar. I know that mistakes of scholarship and of argumentation are made by the best of us, and can be easily forgiven and overlooked. But, as you know, calumny and slander, far from being "mistakes," are grave sins. I went to the book with the intention of taking it seriously, and really

---

[1] My father had sent me a book written by one Dave Hunt, called A Woman Rides the Beast, in hopes that it would show me the error of my ways. A more disgusting, dishonest, and antichrist tome could not be imagined. He had sent it years before to my wife, and to my brother's wife Jessica, to try to convince them not to follow their husbands into the Catholic Church. Not surprisingly, the ladies found the vile screed to be unconvincing. If the reader doubts my personal assessment of the work, he is welcome to do his own research into the matter. He may find that I have been overly generous in my appraisal.

engaging with his claims, for the sake of the truth. I quickly realized (what I had already known from reading him before, but was intentionally forgetting for the sake of doing what you had requested) that Dave Hunt, at least in his "scholarship," personifies the propagandist who has absolutely no regard for the truth whatsoever. Or at least, if he has some regard for it, he has taken great care to hide that regard from his reader, so that it never comes out in his work. While re-reading his book, I realized that it would be almost impossible to respond to, because of the sheer number of undocumented claims, half-truths, bizarre and impossible statements, etc. It would simply be an impossible task, or one that would require a massive volume in its own right. I was going to make an effort, however, and just pick a few of his most calumnious claims, and respond to them.

First, I was going to concede anything he had to say about the "new church" and "popes" that Mr. Hunt erroneously associates with the Catholic Church. He can have all that, and say whatever he likes about it. He is right in that regard precisely because he is wrong. Then I was going to emphasize his absolute disdain for footnoting his incredible claims about the actual Catholic Church, his calling known and public apostates or excommunicates "Catholic historians"(!), and his utter ignorance of pretty much every theological and historical thing he is talking about (one of my favorites was his claim that Saint Robert Bellarmine had no response to those who attacked the Papacy! Perhaps he is unaware that St. Bellarmine, sometimes called the 'Doctor of the Papacy,' wrote a massive tome defending the Papacy on every level from the attacks of the Protestants? Or, could it be, that he didn't actually read Bellarmine's book because it was written in Latin, which is one of the several relevant ancient languages with which Hunt has zero facility, and has only recently been translated into English?). I was going to talk about his strange hatred for those brave Catholics who shed their blood defending Europe and the Holy land from the barbarous Muslims, (he has absolutely poisoned the well for you, by the way, in terms of the history of Christendom, if you take even one word of what he said seriously). I was all geared up to begin the work...

But then I did an Internet search on Dave Hunt's name, just to get a background on him. And, lo and behold, some of the first things to come up were a couple of open letters to Mr. Hunt, written not by Catholics, but by fellow Protestants. You mentioned the book Hunt wrote, attacking some Calvinist position to which he takes exception, if you recall? I am not interested in the particulars of their theological squabble, of course, but I was struck by what at least two of his fellow anti-Catholics said about him and his scholarship, as these relate to that particular anti-Calvinist book. Indeed, everything that I thought while reading <u>A Woman Rides the Beast</u>, these two men put into words, except in relation to some Calvinist theology instead of the Catholic question! Just insert "Catholic Church" in the place of "Calvin" or "Calvinism." I have appended the most relevant portions of their open letters below, along with the links to where the originals can be found. The author of the longest and most devastating piece is James White, who could never be accused of a love for anything Catholic.[2] I bolded and underlined a few of the most devastating statements. You might want to glance at them, and then think about whether Hunt should be considered a reliable source of anything. The destiny of our souls might depend on whether we follow someone like him, or whether we, in fact, flee from people like him. I think there is a proverbial saying in this regard: something about "the blind leading the blind…"[3] You and I have no intention of remaining blind, if we can help it, so let's not follow blind guides.[4]

---

[2] James White is a Calvinist theologian, well known for his hatred of the Catholic Church.
[3] Mathew 15:14
[4] I have decided not to include the portions of the "open letter" in this current publication. Those interested will be able to find it online very easily. They were merely meant to document, to my father's satisfaction, the fact that

Having put aside Hunt, I turned to the website that you recommended. It is indeed far better than Hunt in just about every possible way.[5] It took me only a few minutes online to find various rebuttals and counter rebuttals to his particular claims, but I don't think any kind of detailed response on my part would be helpful. Of anti-Catholic claims there is no end, and any counter claims that I could put forward would have no effect. Further, you are not looking for rebuttals, and neither do you want to start a debate. You are trying to demonstrate that what I have found concerning the Vatican II church is just as true for the Catholic Church through the ages. This premise of yours is unfounded, but I do think that this brings up some larger points that I would like to sort of think through, and am using this present letter as an excuse to do so.

Upon consideration, I realized that I have probably not made myself clear at all over the last decade. In the recent email to mom, I wondered out loud why you don't seem to listen to what I am saying, but then, after our phone call, I

---

even Mr. Hunt's fellow Protestants have had occasion to criticize his dishonest scholarship.

[5] I don't actually remember much about this website, except that it involved more tedious proof-texting, I think with some quotes from St. Augustine instead of the Bible; part of an endless attempt to find a Protestant twig in the Catholic Forest; something historical upon which to hang the novel, *sola* beliefs. But it was certainly more learned and presumably more honest than the Dave Hunt book.

realized, not for the first time, that I am your son. And being your son, I also suffer from an inability to communicate what I am thinking, and especially when it comes to the faith. Jamiey, my long-suffering wife, has let me know that I sometimes have an off-putting tone when I talk about these things. Could it be, I thought to myself, not that dad refuses to listen to everything I tell him, but rather that the substance of what I am trying to convey is impeded by the messenger, who shares many of Dad's same faults (and fewer of his virtues)? This seems likely.

With this in mind, I thought it might be worthwhile to begin at the beginning, and to tell you again why I became Catholic, and why it is that I can never leave the Church that Christ founded. Jamiey also suggested that it might be a good idea. So, what follows is another long and meandering personal narrative. You probably have nothing better to do than to read seventy more pages of Drew's disorganized thoughts... Ha. If you do take the time to read through it, however, I would love to know your thoughts in turn.

The Beginning

Wisdom is seeing the whole, and then seeing how the various parts fit into the whole; and the fear of the Lord is the beginning of wisdom. To know our first cause and last end, and to order our lives in light of those realities is to live a life of wisdom. It is necessary, then, to get a wide-angle view of the whole, in order to understand the tiny sliver of the real that we occupy. This is why I have always been attracted to philosophy, especially to metaphysics, because I want to go straight to the root to find the first causes, and to see the foundations upon which everything else depends. For instance, I want to know what the strongest motives to believe that God exists (and thus could reveal himself), on the natural plane, might be. And the harmony between metaphysics and Revelation is absolutely marvelous in this regard, because God is the author of both. They are both manifestations of the mind of God, through His effects. And grace is a created effect of God, perhaps the greatest effect, as far as we are presently concerned. To understand the world, we need to be able to trace the movements of grace through history, to see it with supernatural eyes, as it were. Further, and more to the point, we need to see the sweep and drama of our own lives in that wider movement of grace; God condescends to deal with the whole, and with the parts. What follows then is an attempt to see the part that is Drew Emmans' 36 years of existence, and to place that small part into the wider river of God's unimaginable love. For my life has been nothing less than a testimony to that fact that Saint John, the Beloved Disciple, explicitly noted: *Deus caritas est.*[6]

To begin: I wonder why it is, in your mind, that I would find the claims of the Catholic Church so convincing? Why do you think I became Catholic in the first place? Catholicism is obviously not an easier path. The Church requires far, far more from its faithful than does any form of Protestantism. Also, I bought it, so to speak, at a very dear cost. This high cost included the loss of family unity, the disdain of my father, mother, pastor, mentors, and most of my friends, and even, at the beginning, the unity of my own family. Jamiey did not follow me into the Church for five or so years, if you recall, and there was never any guarantee that

---

[6] 1 John 4:8 "God is Love."

she would follow at all. Why endure such personal loss and suffering when, according to you and Dave Hunt, it is just a matter of cracking open a Bible, or thumbing through a popular history, to see the myriad errors?

Even now I have to suffer for the faith, as I have realized that I had been mistaken in identifying the Catholic Church with the antichrist's church of Vatican II. I have been forced to give up the hope of a PhD, and the dream of teaching at a Catholic University. You might think this a small thing, but I assure you that for me it is not. There are also very dear friends of ours at Ave Maria with whom our bond of friendship, developed over these last eight years, is irreparably damaged.[7] Further, I had met many and befriended some of the most noteworthy "conservative Catholics" in the Vatican II church, during our time at Ave Maria, theologians and writers, and had what I thought was the great privilege of meeting various conservative "Bishops." I have been inside the walls of the Vatican, and it was almost a guarantee that I would have eventually met the "pope," which was a dream of

---

[7] Ave Maria is a community in South West Florida, built around my *alma mater*, the *Novus Ordo* catholic Ave Maria University. We moved to this community in 2008, a year or so after I became Catholic. I owe a debt of gratitude to both the university and to the town that I could never repay. It was the best thing we could have done for our family. In God's mercy and providence, he took the terrible mistake of falling for the antichrist lies of the *Novus Ordo*, and made Ave Maria a time of growth for our family in ways we could have never imagined.

mine. At Ave, we found ourselves in a very unique and exciting position within the "conservative wing" of the new church. We just kind of fell into it all, and we were poised to "do something" within the new church structures, that is, to become active within its intellectual circles, and participate in what I thought was the promotion of the Kingdom of God. It was certainly more than I could have ever asked for, and we gave it all up. We simply walked away. Why would we do this, for something that you say is so obviously a semi-pagan lie? Why would we choose to suffer like this, for something that is no more than one great statement of blasphemy?

Perhaps you might say that I have merely been deceived, maybe by a smooth-tongued, heretical apologist for the semi-pagans. Very well, I concede the possibility. But then why were Nathan, Jordan, Jamiey and Jess also so easily deceived?[8] Why does mom also find the claims of the Church so convincing? Are we all such fools that we would be led astray by something so obviously opposed to everything we have always believed? Do we all have such a weak and superficial faith (not to mention intellect) that we would throw out our Blessed Lord and Savior Jesus Christ, and then begin

---

[8] My older brother Jordan, my younger brother Nathan, and Nathan's wife Jessica, had all joined the Catholic Church at the time I had written this letter. Jordan had also embraced the *sedevacantist* position at the time I penned the above words.

worshiping demons and other creatures, instead of the Creator, as Dave Hunt has assured you that we do? Why would we all fall *en masse* for the same obvious lie?

Or perhaps you think I enjoy being different and rebellious. I have been accused of these character flaws many times in the past. It seems like a plausible explanation; "You knew Catholicism would make your Father mad," they told me, "So you thought it would be really cool to become Catholic, just like you thought it would be really cool and rebellious to grow your hair out in that ridiculous and un-stylish mess (so Grandma Shirley has helpfully described it)." Dreadlocks and Catholicism go hand in hand. I would very much like to reassure you in this regard. Rebellious is the last thing in the world that I want to be. The demons were rebellious. My whole being finds the *non serviam* of the original rebels repellent in every respect. On the contrary, I have tried, though I have sometimes failed, to be assiduously conscious of the "first commandment with a promise." Neither my ridiculous "hairstyle" nor my religion is founded on rebellion. I would rather follow Chesterton's advice, to "break the conventions and keep the commandments."

Related to this is the possibility of pride. I enjoy being different, perhaps, as some kind of show of pride. Perhaps I am too proud to merely worship as my fathers have worshiped, or to believe as I was taught. No, according to this hypothesis, I have to be unique, to be different, even if it means blaspheming God and worshiping demons. Thus, I proudly disdained the faith in which I was raised, and became Catholic. And now I refuse to even look at the claims of the Catholic Church in a critical way, because I am too proud to admit that I erred in becoming Catholic in the first place. I heap pride upon pride to my own damnation.

This too seems plausible. Pride is a great snare for the soul, and a snare into which, for reasons that need no elaboration, the Emmans men are especially prone to fall. I confess to being proud in many ways, and in many areas of thought and life. I do not deny it. But this moral failing has *never* been a motive for becoming Catholic. No, rather, I became Catholic precisely to reject the very pride that severed our Protestant fathers from the one true Church. I reject the pride involved in thinking that I, Drew Emmans, can figure out on my own every detail of Christianity by merely reading the Bible. I reject the pride of refusing obedience to those to whom Christ Himself entrusted the Church, "the pillar and bulwark of the truth."[9] I utterly contemn and abhor the pride

---

[9] 1 Timothy 3:15

of promoting or adhering to theological *novelty*, including the guiding principle and first premise of Protestantism: the principle of *private judgment*. But there is for me one motive for pride, and one in whom I do boast: in our Blessed Lord and Savior Jesus Christ, who has guided this proud, sinful, and utterly worthless man to His one true Church, *extra ecclesiam nulla salus est.*

No, the motive for becoming Catholic is not found in any of these places. I locate the beginning, rather, in the earliest years of my childhood. There is a memory that I have, one upon which I have long pondered and meditated, although I have never shared it. I was perhaps three or five years old, certainly no older than this, when I first heard the dogma of *hell*. I lay that night writhing in my bed for what seemed like hours, in our corner room in Lincoln, in very real existential agony, begging God not to let me go to hell. I prayed and prayed, knowing nothing more about what I was doing than that I was terrified of hell. At that moment the real possibility of losing the Pearl of Great Price was seared into my consciousness, even though I did not know what the Pearl itself might be. I prayed that night as I have never prayed before or since. And God answers prayers.

I have never talked about that particular memory, because to do so would seem to presume upon God's mercy, as though I were already safely home. But this is where it all begins.

Throughout my childhood our particular brand of Protestantism was the air I breathed. Never did I entertain a real doubt about the Divinity of our Lord, or the Divine inspiration of Sacred Scripture. *And I believed it because both you and mom lived your lives as though it all were true.* Even, as a teenager, when I thought to myself, "I don't have to believe anything my parents tell me about God," I would immediately tell myself: "yes, except that I know it is true."

Mom told us over and over again, growing up, that Jesus is the Truth, and that truth can never contradict truth. There is never reason to fear that a real contradiction to the faith will come from science, or from philosophy. There are an almost infinite number of errors to avoid, of course, but God is the author of all truth. It all belongs to God. Indeed, you reminded me of this fact when I first brought to you my concerns about our Protestant heritage, if you recall. I have carried this assurance with me all these 36 years. Never have I been actually worried that an argument against the faith did not have an answer, even if I did not necessarily know every answer to every objection. I really did love the truth, and I really did want to live a life in the truth. You and mom told us over and over again to pursue truth, to follow the truth, wherever He would lead.

To return to my childhood, there are a number of small anecdotes that I want to share, which I think are important. At least, they are important to me, when I survey the life I have so far lived.

I first heard the word Catholic when I was maybe eight or nine years old, and asked mom what Catholicism was. Unless I am conflating two separate conversations, she said that we were all Catholics at one point, but that the Catholics developed a bunch of problems, which were subsequently corrected during the Reformation. We were no longer Catholics because the Catholics were no longer Christians. Something like that... I considered that description to be the gospel truth for many years. It was the definition that I brought to mind when it first hit me like a bolt of lightning that the Catholic Church might be the only way to square the various circles that I had run into as a youth pastor.

The Bible was, for the whole Emmans family, Christianity. The two were coterminous. I remember hearing many times that we attended a "Bible-believing church." I was shocked by the implication that anyone would actually go to a church that *didn't* believe the Bible. It didn't make any sense. I assumed at the time that believing the Bible had a specific content that was univocally the same for every church that did, in fact, believe the Bible. There were only two options then: either a Bible-believing Church, or a church that did not believe the Bible. What insanity to go to the latter.

I recall one sermon preached by Pastor Tim, in which he said something to the effect that, "don't ever just believe what I am telling you! Always go compare it to the Word of God, to see if it is true!"[10] I thought to myself, "then why on earth do we have to come to church every Sunday to hear you yak on about stuff? Good grief, if we can't even trust you, what is the point? I thought you were giving us something we couldn't get on our own. If I have to go read it for myself anyway, just to make sure you are not making things up, why not skip the middle man?" A childish thought, perhaps, but one weighted with significance.

Pastor Kent once said that he was so glad that God gave us nothing physical, nothing tangible in relation to our

---

[10] Tim K. was the Pastor of the church in which I spent my formative years, Cool Community Church.

faith.[11] He said that if God had given us something physical, we would have made an idol out of it. I thought to myself at the time, "wow, I really wish God *had* given us something tangible! It would make things so much clearer and accessible." Of course, I was not able to articulate at the time what I instinctively felt, but now I realize that God did indeed give us physical and tangible elements for practicing the True Religion, precisely because we are not purely spiritual beings. Our religion is based on God becoming man. The Incarnation is precisely a composite reality! We are naturally, unlike God and the Angels, composite beings. We are composed of matter and form, the spiritual and the physical. And that is our natural mode of existence! We affirm the "resurrection of the body" in the creed, because that is exactly what is going to happen. God made us a composite, and the Second Person of the Blessed Trinity Himself *became* a composite in the Incarnation. So, when I discovered that Christianity really does have so many elements that are composite, namely the Sacraments, I realized how well it all fit. Baptism is a physical washing that is specified by words to effect, by the power of the Holy Spirit, a *spiritual* washing, in which our sins, both original and personal, are absolutely made pure. Our soul is *really* made clean by water and the

---

[11] Pastor Kent was the assistant pastor at Cool Community Church.

word. It is not an allegory, or a cheap metaphor of "dung and snow." It really happens.

Anyway, these are various memories that might seem scattered and pointless to you, but they are all connected, at least in my mind. We used to read our Bibles every morning before school, as you probably recall. During those times I would come across so many verses that seemed to oppose what we were taught at church or AWANA, or wherever.[12] I read, for instance, that apostles were given the power and authority to *forgive sins*. How could that be, I wondered at the time? What did it mean, and how did it fit? I remember Keith Green's song about the sheep and the goats, and I remember at the end of that song, he said: "And my friends, the only difference between the sheep and the goats, according to the scriptures, is what they did and didn't *do*!"[13] I knew he was just quoting scripture with his song, but I thought to myself, "doesn't that contradict everything else I hear about salvation being by faith alone, and not by works of any kind?"

---

[12] AWANA: Approved Workmen Are Not Ashamed. This is a program designed to help children and youths to be better Protestant Christians. I believe it is still used in various denominations today.

[13] Keith Green was an early Christian rock musician, during the 1970's. He died young in a tragic plane crash in 1982. As a child, his records would play in our home, and the song quoted above is very familiar to my family.

Further, as an aside, I would like to point out that your own life testifies against your Protestant beliefs. You live your own life, and you taught us in no uncertain terms, that what we *did* mattered for salvation, even if you insisted with your words that it was all faith, and no works. It is absolutely convoluted and a contradiction. You don't practice what you preach! I knew it even at the time, although I couldn't put an exact finger on the issue at stake.

Also, you read the <u>Lord of the Rings</u> to us, when we were young. It would be hard to overstate the effect that book had on me. Wide vistas were opened up for me, and I saw the whole drama of the Catholic faith hidden in a fantastic story. I do not overstate things when I say that Tolkien was absolutely instrumental in the faith I maintained as a youth, and in my subsequent conversion to the Catholic Church. I remember thinking as a young man, "it is too bad that Tolkien was Catholic. His books are so Christian!" In this regard, I remember hearing that Tolkien had actually been instrumental in the conversion of the atheist C.S. Lewis, another of my childhood heroes. Strange that he could convert him to some form of Christianity, when he himself was just another dupe of the antichrist.

As a child and young man, I often wondered why Christianity seemed so *thin*. That is, why, after two thousand years, we had no real history to speak of? Occasionally we would get a glimpse of something bigger, like when mom taught her Church history classes at Cool Community Church, but it was occasional, and always sort of prefaced by a certain distaste for the history of the Church. There was sometimes mention of the very earliest Christians, and their heroic martyrdoms at the hands of the Romans, but then the history of the Church would sort of...cloud over. The next thing we knew was that Luther was unshackling the Bible from the dark tower of the Inquisition (or whatever), where it had been imprisoned for one thousand years. Here I exaggerate, if only slightly, to make the point. I consciously wondered why we knew nothing of our history, and why there were not more heroes of the faith given to us as models of virtue and behavior. You might think I am projecting my later thoughts onto my childhood, but I assure you I am not. These were conscious, explicit thoughts. There was a curious *thinness* to our faith, historically (and philosophically, but this I realized later). Thinness is how I described it to myself all those years ago. Although all truth was supposedly ours, we sure did not act like it. Why this strange reluctance to speak of the truth of the Church's history?

I remember thinking that we had the modern martyr Jim Eliot, and a handful of others, and then this or that famous theologian between the Reformation and the current day, but it was a very thin sample. Before the Reformation, I think the last "true believer" that we knew of was maybe Saint Augustine? Even though he was a monk and Bishop in the Catholic Church, saying Mass every day, we sometimes bizarrely claim him as a Protestant, I think because Calvin and Luther wanted to claim him. Mom even had some books of his on the shelf. Even when talking about the Crusades, for instance, and the glorious struggle to defend Europe and Christendom from the barbarous Muslims, there was a great reluctance to affirm them unreservedly (people like Hunt categorically condemn them). They had crosses on their shields, and fought for Christendom, but they weren't "Christians." I asked mom about the paucity of "true Christians" during the strange, extended historical void, and she said something to the effect of: "Well, there have always been true believers, even during those times. But they are hard to find. You have to follow the 'trail of blood' to find them. That is, you have to find out where people were being martyred in those times, and that's where the true believers were." I think that mom ceased believing this bit of historical fiction years and years ago, but she did believe it once.[14]

There were many of these sorts of memories from my childhood. I share them with you in an attempt to show you something of what I see when I survey, in my mind's eye, the sweep of my life until now. Whether to hear these random memories now is meaningful or helpful to you I don't know. But from where I sit, they are incredibly important. God was even then, from the earliest moments of my existence, giving grace, and even then answering my prayers, and your prayers on my behalf.

To continue: When I reached my late high school and early college years, I fell into a sort of petty and ugly rebellion against God. I never for a minute disbelieved in Him, but I rather simply ignored Him. I literally thought to myself, to my eternal shame, that I would wait to "take my faith seriously," until I was older, maybe 25 or 30. What a fool I was! And God allows us to be fools, if we insist on it. Once during my self-imposed slide into darkness, I was driving along highway

---

[14] My mother has told me since that she does not remember this conversation, or ever believing this! Perhaps she had mentioned it only as something that some people believed...

80 to some event or other and I realized that I had not even *thought* about God for over a month...

During this time, I attended church sporadically, and I knew deep down that if I were to die, I would not go to heaven. No matter what people would say about "faith alone," and the impossibility of losing one's "salvation," etc., I knew that God was not mocked. He would by no means say to me, "*Well done, thou good and faithful servant.*"[15] Indeed, it was my beloved wife who was the instrumental cause of pulling me out of this mire. Even early in our marriage I didn't want to go to church, and I found every excuse to miss it. But, at her urging, I began again to think about God, to read the Bible, to pray, if still only very infrequently, and to go to church. It was a dark time spiritually, and one that was absolutely self-imposed.

With Jamiey's help I began to turn again to our Blessed Lord and Savior Jesus Christ. Isaiah was born, and never have I felt greater joy, or a greater sense of weight of responsibility before God like I did the first time I held him.[16] This brand-new soul was of such great value that the Second Person of the ever-Blessed Trinity would Himself even die on

---

[15] Mathew 25:23
[16] The eldest of our nine children, seven sons and two daughters. I am wealthy far beyond my merit.

the Cross for his sake, and this little boy had been entrusted to *my* temporal and spiritual care. He was born with his eyes open, and looking right at me...

Then we acquired *Isidor's Coffee and Tea.*[17] It was for us an adventure of epic proportion, and one that I mishandled as badly as I have mishandled anything. This was not due to incompetence (or not exclusively!), but rather to sin. I ignored God, and made some business decisions that I will always regret. Instead of being obedient, I decided to allow my pride to dictate the way we ran our business, and I was very severely rebuked by God. But God reproves and chastises those whom He loves.

I have never been so low temporally or spiritually. There were also other factors. At the coffee shop I was surrounded daily by sodomites, communists, drug addicts, atheists, metal head death-worshipers, and various haters-of-God of every stripe. It was incredibly draining, and dark. Their hatred for Christianity in particular was causing me great angst, and that, combined with my own barren spiritual life, had a debilitating effect on me. Satan was taking every advantage of my flight from God. But during this particularly

---

[17] A coffee shop in downtown Sacramento, CA. It was the first of our big adventures.

difficult time, there was a moment of tremendous light. You and mom had given each of us a copy of Chesterton's Orthodoxy, if you recall, for Christmas one year. It sat on my shelf for several years, until I was at this low point. I read it at the coffee shop when I could manage it, and it was like a breeze from some far distant country, free and clean, blowing through the dark and barren places of my mind. The effect was almost indescribable; I no longer felt the weight of the all the hatred of God around me. The freshness, force, and beautiful rationality of Christianity came rushing through once again. Indeed, so great was the effect on me, that I do not hesitate to state, hyperbolically, that G.K. Chesterton saved my soul. He was the instrumental cause that God used for my conversion, both back to God at that moment, and ultimately to the Catholic Church.

Also, at Nathan's suggestion, I read Thomas Merton's 7 Story Mountain. It had an interesting effect on me as well. Although I knew next to nothing about Catholicism, I found his description of Catholic life and faith to be moving and poetic. Indeed, to be Christian! It was an aesthetical experience, rather than an intellectual one. I didn't think much of it at the time, except that it was unexpected. It may have occurred to me at the time also to remember that Tolkien himself was Catholic.

So it was that we come to what I consider the turning point of my entire life. Here, during the darkness brought on by my own flight from God, God extended to me grace. He made me see what I had become, and gave me a glimpse of what I would inevitably be if I continued in this petty rebellion. *"It is hard for thee to kick against the goad..."*[18] I prayed a prayer then that I will never forget. I begged for forgiveness, and I promised God that I would obey Him from then on, for the rest of my life. I said explicitly that I would go wherever He asked me to go, and that I would do whatever He asked me to do, *no matter what the cost,* and no matter how much it hurt. I meant that prayer with all my heart.

I took the most labor-intensive job I could find that summer, as an act of penance for my sins, even though I did not know what penance was. And by the end of that summer, God began to move again in the Emmans family.

---

[18] Acts 26:14

The Deluge

Celebration Community Fellowship, the church we had been attending, came to us and asked us to help out with the youth group. Please believe me when I tell you that I had no desire whatsoever to help out in that regard. I did not like high school students, and I despised their destructive "youth culture." I did not think that I would be a good fit at all. I almost said no. But I remembered my promise to God, and being as convinced as a person can be without having had a direct revelation from God that it was God's will, I said yes, even though I would have rather done just about anything else.

We threw ourselves into the task. We opened our home to those kids, and did everything we could do to convince them that God was real, that He became man, and dwelt among us. We suffered, prayed, studied, organized events, had interventions with kids and parents, dealt with kids going to jail, and everything else associated with that kind of ministry. It was very difficult, but by the grace of God we had some success. However, I went into the job with open eyes in this respect: *that God would require an account of what I taught those kids about the faith.* I do not hesitate to put it this strongly, namely, that the fear of God was on me. I remembered St. James' warning, the same one I relayed in my letter to our Ave friends, which I paraphrase thus: "*don't everyone rush out to be teachers, because a teacher is accountable to God for the souls of his students, and incurs a greater judgment.*"[19] So, I began to get books on being a pastor, what it meant, and what was required, because I knew that God is not mocked.

Then came the event that triggered the deluge.

Our immediate bosses and mentors (whom we loved then and love now), Larry and Carol, decided that all the youth staff would go to an event in Los Angeles.[20] It was a

---

[19] James 3:1 This quotation was included in an open letter that I had written to our friends in Ave Maria, after we had moved, informing them of our leaving the *Novus Ordo* religion, and becoming *sedevacantist*, traditional Catholics. I also sent the letter to my parents and siblings. However, I erroneously attributed the quote to St. Paul, both in the letter and in the lecture at the Fatima Conference.

[20] Larry and Carol D. were not only our mentors, but some of the most kind and generous people we have ever met. Carol was extremely protective of my wife Jamiey, and of our little kiddos, and went well out of her way to ensure that our work for Celebration Community Fellowship did not cause a strain on our marriage. When we moved to Florida, after my initial conversion to what I erroneously believed to be the Catholic Church, I drove out with our worldly possessions a week or so before Jamiey followed with the kiddos. During that

conference for youth pastors, not youth groups. So about six of us flew down for four or five days for the conference; Jamiey couldn't come with us, I think because of the kiddos.

It was the kind of thing that had a big performance by well-known bands in the evenings, and various speakers, etc. There were thousands of youth pastors there from every conceivable denomination, and the whole point of it was to re-energize and reinvigorate youth pastors, as well as give them tools to better carry out their ministry. During the day there were various workshops and talks on different topics, given by different experts or authors, and the pastors could attend some or none of them, depending on their needs and interests. Our group decided to go to a couple of talks on "postmodernism," which was a subject that had come up before in various contexts at Celebration.

We went to two workshops that fateful day. The first was very interesting, given by a guy who had written a book on the subject whose name escapes me. He suggested that postmodernism was a fact that youth pastors had to deal with, so we should modify the various methods by which we shared

---

very difficult time, Larry and Carol had Jamiey and the kids stay with them, and Carol made sure that Jamiey was able to simply rest. Jamiey told me that their kindness was one of the only things that kept her sane during that traumatic transition.

the gospel. It was analogous to going to a foreign country, and learning the particular intellectual framework within which the natives viewed the world, and acting accordingly. The substance was by no means affected; just the particular methods were adapted. I thought this to be a reasonable approach to the question.

It was the next workshop that was decisive. It was formatted as a debate between I think four various pastors and "experts" on the subject, moderated by the same guy who gave the talk that morning. It was one of the most disturbing things I had heretofore encountered.

As these things often go, the guy with the biggest personality commands the most attention. The debate was on the best way to deal with the postmodernism amongst youths, but ended up being an indictment of something called the "institutional church." The Big Personality (BP), as I will call him for our purposes, gave us his "testimony." Unlike the earlier workshop, the issue was not that we needed to change some various strategies for dealing with a new situation, but *rather that the "institutional church" needed to change, because it had utterly lost its ability to be credible, and abandoned its "New Testament roots."* BP said that he was once the assistant pastor at some huge mega church, maybe in Texas, and that he was constantly speaking out against the unbiblical institutional mindset of his church, and basically causing a righteous ruckus. Finally, someone told him that, if he was so bothered by everything going on in his church, he should (wait for it) go start his own church! BP thought that was an excellent idea, and proceeded to do so. He told us, very proudly, how he had created the new paradigm, which he insisted was really the old, Biblical paradigm, for "doing church." Thus, he invented what I dubbed, "The Church of Chaos."

At the beginning of this new church, he said, he gathered a group of people into his living room, to talk about how to go about it (don't you know, this is exactly how all the "New Testament" churches started?). The people were, if my memory serves me, made up primarily of those who had very recently made some kind of faith profession. So, BP asked them: "What should we call our church?" They looked at each other, and said something to the effect of, "Why do we need a name?" You see, being new "converts," they were pure, and had not been tainted by all the un-Biblical trappings of the institutional church. "Ok," said BP, "that sounds reasonable. I guess I have been so caught up in the 'institutional church,' that I just assumed you had to have a name. So, no name then. What about opening a bank account, how should we do that?" His living room guests responded, "Why do we need a bank account?" And then, "What about a building?" The predictable response: "Why do we need a building?" Soon, he described his Church of Chaos to us, with all the pride of a new father: "We don't have a name, and we don't have any hierarchy. We take turns either giving a Bible study, or a talk, or sharing some thoughts that the *spirit* inspires. We don't meet every Sunday, or even every week necessarily. We just send some emails out saying when we are meeting, and where. Sometimes we go to a park to feed the homeless, and once (my personal favorite) we went to a Mosque!" Here he looked at all of us with some condescension, as though he could tell that we were all a bunch of rubes who didn't go to Mosques. He didn't say *why* he went to the Mosque, but I didn't get the impression that it was to evangelize.

It would be hard to overstate how disturbed this talk left me. There was much more to it then I have shared, of course, but that is the main thrust, and that is what has stayed with me all these years. I was shaken to the core, and I said so to Larry and Carol, as we were all talking about it afterwards. I thought that it was madness, insanity, and chaos. How could something like this be recommended to us at a conference like this? (I do want to hasten to add that the majority of those present at the debate, including the other panelists, probably had the same reaction that I had). But then, I thought to myself, maybe the problem is not in what he said, but in the fact that I am a product of the "institutional church," and can't see past my own bias. Maybe the problem is in me. But, I said, not to worry! I know exactly where to go to get a definitive answer: to the Bible.

You will suspect at this point that I am a credulous *naïf.* You yourself have long known of the chaos that pervades the Protestant world, and you know that it is not possible to just "go to the Bible" to find definitive answers to this or any ecclesiological question. But I truly did not know. I should have known, I think, because I had been given plenty of opportunity to face this reality in the past, but I didn't. Sometimes we just don't see what is all around us and right in front of us until we do, in fact, see it. I honestly thought that we all essentially believed the same things, except perhaps in things like what kind of music we preferred on Sunday morning. I thought, as I mentioned above, that "Bible-believers" was a category with an actual content beyond simply a nebulous "belief." I assumed it meant that we all believed the *same things* about the Bible. So, when I say that I really thought I could simply go to the Bible to resolve this issue, I really did think I could do it. It is just a matter of studying what the Bible says about the Church and her structure. I little knew where such a task would lead.

This event was some time in the summer, if memory serves, and I started at William Jessup University that fall. I began to look into ecclesiology, and into the nature of the Church. It was then that I ran immediately into the issue of "denominations." I had always supposed, again, that the main thing about denominations was aesthetical considerations, or the particular charism of the founder, or something like that. I did not realize then, although I quickly found out, that they all believe things that impinge on the substance of the faith that are diametrically opposed to each other. But wait, I said to myself, this cannot be. How can everyone believe such radically different things about Christianity? And about the *basics* of the faith, not some obscure theological question with no formal connection to the salvation of souls. There had to be a way to bridge this gap.

I began to pay close attention to the variations while at my university. The "diversity" was appalling to me. I began to grow very concerned about what I was teaching my kids. How could I be sure that I wasn't leading them astray? You will recall how this concern had already taken root in my soul, through the warning of Saint Paul. And things kept coming up that forced the question. I remember a conversation I had with Pastor Cedric, about a marriage he had recently conducted.[21] I can't remember the point he was trying to make by telling me about it, but I do remember the effect it had on me. He had just officiated at the marriage of a young couple, and the young man in question had been married before. He and his first wife were divorced soon after, and it was chalked up to a youthful indiscretion kind of thing. But the father of this young man was also a pastor, and he had *refused* to officiate at the marriage of the new couple, because of the young man's previous marriage. But Pastor Cedric had no problem performing the task. I asked Pastor Cedric, "How is it that both of you are Christian Pastors, who both take the Bible as the sole rule of faith, and one of you refuse to do something that impinges directly on the faith, and has been spoken about innumerable times in the Bible, while the other has no problem doing it? Which one of you is right? What if, pastor Cedric, you are wrong in this regard?" He told me, "Drew, when I stand before God someday, if He says, 'Cedric, why did you marry those two? That was wrong.' I will tell Him, 'I didn't know...'" I was shocked. How can we not know? Two thousand years, and we still don't know the *basics*

---

[21] Cedric L. was the pastor of Celebration Community Fellowship, and my boss.

of Christian morality? But if adultery is a grave sin, and adulterers don't inherit the kingdom, as the Bible clearly states, shouldn't we be *really* sure that we are not complicit in adultery? How can we be so cavalier about sins of this gravity? *What's more, how can someone who claims for himself the title "shepherd of souls," or pastor, be so cavalier?* How can the shepherd "not know" about something of such immediate and formal connection to the salvation of his sheep?

But of course, most Protestants do not believe that we have to avoid grave sins anyway. They might say that we *should* avoid grave sin, but not that we *must*, if we want to be saved. All past and *all future* sins were forgiven when we "accepted Jesus," as Dan K. once told me, to name just one of myriad instances.[22] Most Protestants would literally not understand the questions as I posed them above. Most or many Protestants think that we do not even have to obey the Ten Commandments. As long as we have "faith," we will still go to heaven, while treading the commandments of God underfoot. I know there are exceptions to this, including you and Mom, but that is the whole point. Should I believe Dad's

---

[22] Dan K. was one of my youth pastors through high school, and the father of my best friend. He had a great influence on me in my youth, and I always considered him to be something of a mentor.

critical exegesis of the Bible in this regard, or Dr. John Piper's, for instance?[23]

There were so many other instances like this. In our little community of Meadow Vista there were five churches. I asked our mentors, "why don't we join forces with our youth groups (kind of like mom suggested to the missionaries in Bolivia!)?"[24] "Well, of course," they answered, "we can't do that, because we don't really know what they teach or believe (!)." What, aren't they all *Bible-believing* Christians? How can we not know what they all believe? It should be *exactly* what we believe. That is what the phrase *"one faith"* is all about!

At the time I also thought, in my naiveté, that heresy was something definable in Protestantism. Part of this credulity could not be culpably imputed, however. I accepted it on authority! I remember Mom telling us when we were kids about a conversation at Cool Community Church that she had, when teaching her classes on Church history. A gentleman who was at her class was giving his definition of the Trinity, if memory serves me, and it was one that had been

[23] Dr. John Piper is a noted Baptist Theologian and pastor.
[24] My parents and my baby sister Lydia lived for three years in Bolivia, after my father retired. They spent their time there helping a Protestant missionary group, and my mother taught at the missionary school. My mom told me how she had suggested combining forces with other missionary groups in the area for some end, and had received the above reply.

condemned by the Catholic Church as heresy. Mom pointed this out to him, saying something like, "Actually, that definition has been condemned as heresy." That conversation stayed with me all those years, and contributed to my naïve supposition that (Protestant) Christianity had a specified content, and that there existed an authority that could, in fact, "condemn." But who can "condemn" a definition of the Trinity? Who has that authority or power? No one, and no body, has that authority within the confines of the Protestant error. And heresy can only be defined in relation to orthodoxy, and that in turn can only be defined if there is a univocal content to faith, and an authority to say definitively what it is. That is, unless heresy and orthodoxy be nothing more than a meaningless game of semantics. Heresy and orthodoxy are in this way just two sides of the same coin, so to speak. And the only authority that can command the will in all things that impinge upon the salvation of our souls is a Divine Authority. But in Protestantism, your heresy is my orthodoxy, and my heresy is your orthodoxy, and the voice of authority that pretends to speak is merely the cacophony of Babel, an endless and impotent argument proffered by self-proclaimed "shepherds" over the texts of Sacred Scripture.

In this regard, I remember thumbing through a book that Nathan had been reading at California Baptist University, entitled <u>Heresy</u>. This may have been after I became Catholic, or just before, I can't remember. It was something of a history of heresy, from the early Church to today, if I remember correctly. But it was the final conclusion that the author drew that stayed with me. He said (a rough paraphrase), "It is impossible any longer to define heresy, because there is no longer an authoritative body capable of calling a general council." This author was a Protestant, presumably a Baptist of some kind, and he correctly concluded that heresy was something that can no longer be defined. He is right, precisely because he is wrong. He imagined that Protestantism is true Christianity rather than simply a mass of comingled heresy, and that the Catholic Church is a semi-pagan corruption of the faith, perhaps even the "whore of Babylon." He is right that Protestantism is absolutely incapable of defining either heresy or orthodoxy. But if heresy could be defined in ages past, what authority was it that did the defining? Whose voice spoke all those centuries ago? Only a Divine voice can command the will in relation to Divine things, then as now. So what voice was it that spoke then? And if a voice spoke then, why doesn't it speak now? If the voice was Divine and could thus command the will, whither did it go? Who silenced it? No, this is an utterly false and irrational supposition. Heresy both still exists and still kills souls, but the same divine authority that spoke in Nicaea, for instance, and at Jerusalem, still speaks today. We can know the content of the faith, and avoid all heresy, if we so choose. The same voice that defined heresy dogmatically all those centuries ago against the perversions and corruptions of the heretics still rings out against the perversions and corruptions of the modern heretics, with all the force of Christ Himself. And this precisely because *it is Christ's own authority* with which the Catholic Church speaks: *"He that heareth you, heareth me; and he that despiseth you, despiseth me; and he that despiseth me, despiseth him that sent me."*[25] The tongues of the heretics were "death dealing" then, and they are "death dealing" now.

Anyway, I began to realize that it was not only BP's church that is the church of chaos; all of Protestantism is a mass of chaos in both doctrine and praxis. Almost all the churches that we have ever attended have been break-away church splits. I do not need to belabor this point. You are very familiar with the scandalous reality of the proliferation of Protestant "denominations." I remember Pastor Cedric's wife telling me once that we at Celebration reject the disunity of the denominations. That's why Celebration is (wait for it) "non-denominational!" The strange thing about this state of

---

[25] Luke 10:16

affairs is that we just take it for granted, as Protestants. We honestly think the "church" has always been this way. But of course, it hasn't. That is, there have always been heresies and schisms, but heresies and schisms *sever those unfortunates involved from the unity of the Church*, and these dead branches will eventually be gathered up to be burned. We as Protestants are just surprised to learn that we trace our spiritual patrimony to one of these dead branches, separated from that vine "apart from which we can do nothing." But the schisms and heresies cannot damage the Church herself. The one unified subject, namely the Church, suffers no harm, except accidently; for instance, today, with the cloud of probably hundreds of thousands of false churches, including and especially the false Vatican II sect, it is very difficult for honest men to find the One True Church. Nevertheless, the Church, as a visible reality, will continue until the end of time, regardless of how small and persecuted she becomes, or how temporally great and magnificent. And all the various schisms, heresies and heresiarches, each diverse in the various aspects of the one faith that each denies or perverts, are united in one regard only. Indeed, they are together united in this one regard with every antichrist power in the world, including the pagans, the Muslims, the Communists, etc.: *they are all united in being opposed to the Catholic Church.* The Church is the immovable rock against which all the various counterfeit churches and theologies break themselves.

I was so disoriented by all this that it is hard to put into words. Everywhere I looked I found doctrinal chaos. What was Christianity? How could I know what a Christian was required to believe or to do? I was given all sorts of answers, of course, but every time the fact of the doctrinal chaos was downplayed or denied. "Don't believe your lying eyes, Drew." And in each instance, it was an arbitrary answer. If it was really true that we agreed on the "basics," or the "fundamentals," then there would be no doctrinal chaos, and I wouldn't be in this situation. Even when someone claimed it was the creed that provided the fundamentals, for instance, they would all interpret the creed in a variety of ways. A friend during this time even told me about some theologian he was reading who argued we should change the phrasing of the Apostles creed, because the current phrasing was open to misinterpretation, according to his particular flavor of Christianity! Change the creed after 2,000 years of Christianity! Not that very many Protestants could recite the creed anyway; I couldn't, at the time.

They said that it was all just about believing in Jesus, that he was the Son of God, and that He died for our sins; but in what does saving "belief" consist? And what about those who also believe that Jesus is the Son of God, and died for our sins, but reject His Divinity, to name but one possible corruption among myriads? "We exclude them," you might say, but on what basis? For instance, your late friend Ron S., *requiem in pace*, confessed that he did not believe in the Divinity of our Lord.[26] Based just on this confession, and bracketing the interior dimension of which God alone is the sovereign Judge, is he in heaven now, or in hell? Based on this public evidence alone? If you say he is in heaven, because he obviously had "belief," and surely "accepted Jesus Christ as his Lord and Savior," and, while being unfortunately in error in this regard, he nevertheless manifested a Christian belief; why then are you concerned that my Catholic beliefs will exclude me from the beatific vision? Surely they meet the minimum qualifications, even in your judgment? Do I not believe in Jesus? Do I not manifest some minimum of Christian belief? Have I not "accepted Jesus Christ as my personal Lord and Savior?" If you say he is a heretic, and

---

[26] Dr. S., a very learned and intelligent man, was a professor at a local Bible College in Sacramento, and a mentor to my parents when they were new Protestant Christians. It was said that he had actually performed miracles; he had a framed newspaper page in his home, attesting to the fact. I have many wonderful memories of watching old movies at his home when I was very young, while my parents were in his living room with my uncle and aunt, and a few other friends, attending a Bible Study. Very sadly he confessed to my mother personally, just before his death, that he had ceased believing in the Divinity of our Blessed Lord, based on his study of the Bible.

therefore excluded from the Kingdom, I then pose two questions: first, how then can you be so cavalier about whether there are not other dogmas, being denied or affirmed or ignored, that might also exclude one from the Kingdom? The second: on what authority do you make that claim? Do you make it on an authority greater than Sacred Scripture, of which the late Dr. S. was considered something of an expert?

It must be stated that I never once doubted that there were answers to the questions I was encountering, never once. I believed then and I believe now in everything that God has revealed, because God has revealed it. And you and Mom have over and over emphasized that our faith is *true*, because our Blessed Lord and Savior Jesus Christ is the Truth. But where could I find answers? How could this problem be solved? I had by then realized that I had to cut to the root, and to look to the first principles. And I soon located the principle involved: authority.

One conversation I had with my pastor put things into stark colors. As a little background, Celebration was a semi-charismatic church, and flirted with a sort of "prosperity gospel." Pastor Cedric told me that he thought that God wanted "believers" to have lots of good things here in this life; material things as in a nice house, nice car, lots of money, etc.

He disliked any kind of "penitential" gospel, although he himself fasted often. During the conversation in question (I don't remember the context), he mentioned that he thought Zwingli right on the question of the "Lord's Supper;" Christ was in no way present, except perhaps in some nebulous, spiritual form. This was opposed to Luther and his "consubstantiation." I cannot remember the details of Zwingli's position, but I seemed to remember that among the most prominent reformers, Zwingli was considered very radical even by his fellow revolutionaries. I mentioned this to Cedric, and asked why he would adopt the more radical position. He smiled, and proceeded to tell me that he considered himself a "new sort of pastor," one that did not follow any one particular "theological system." He was a truly non-denominational pastor. "I take a little of Luther's theology, a little of Calvin, a little of Zwingli, etc." In addition to the original reformers from whom he "took a little of," he also mentioned some contemporary theologians whose names escape me, although they were familiar to me at the time. Cedric really thought that this was a *virtue*, and he really thought he was unique in this regard. Of course, this admission simultaneously destroyed the rule of *sola scriptura,* but as I had already realized by then, Protestantism is incapable of maintaining consistency, because it is built on absolutely false premises (those premises I could not yet identify).

I thought to myself at the time, "but how do we know which, if any, of these various pieces are *true*? Is Pastor Cedric smarter or wiser or better read or more holy than Luther, or any of these others? How can he just pick and choose what he thinks is best? What if he chooses wrong, to the damnation of the souls entrusted to his care?" It was at this point that I realized with horror the end game of Protestantism: *I was just doomed to fall wherever I fell, theologically.* I would end up deciding which of various options was the most appealing to me, and which sounded the most reasonable, and I would become that kind of "Christian." I too, just "took a little of" whomever appealed to me! It was all a big game, and we were all just playing fast and loose with our souls, and the souls of all those entrusted to our care.

This was a shocking realization to me. You see, Dad, I really believed then, as I really believe now, that hell exists, and that it is really a place to which I can be condemned; and it is absolutely relevant to note that there are *many* Protestants who deny the real existence of hell, or who deny that hell is actually occupied by anyone who is not a fallen angel. The agonized childhood prayer that I shared with you at the beginning of this letter was even then in my mind. And I believed then as I believe now, although I could not perhaps articulate it quite this way, that heretics will not inherit the Kingdom of God, and neither will those who die in a state of mortal sin, a sin that leads to death. But if I don't know what Christianity authoritatively teaches, *in every facet of the moral life that impinges on salvation,* then how do I know when I have done some wicked act? *What Christianity authoritatively teaches,* by which I mean having the ability to *command the will,* and not just to manipulate texts? If I do not know, I will wander blindly, and blindly lead my wife and children, and my high school kids. And I will die in my sins, and receive a greater condemnation, *precisely because I appropriated for myself the title of shepherd, of pastor, and of teacher.* If I don't know what Christianity authoritatively says about the nature of God, of our Lord, of His Church, etc., etc., then how do I know if what I tell my family and my high school kids is true or false? How do I know that I am not a heretic? And Dad, how do I know *that I myself am not one of the many false shepherds against whom the Bible repeatedly warns the faithful?*

Further, Saint Peter says: "*As also in all [St. Paul's] epistles, speaking in them of these things; in which are certain things hard to be understood, which the unlearned and unstable wrest, as they do also the other scriptures, to their own destruction. You therefore, brethren, knowing these things before, take heed, lest being led aside by the error of the unwise, you fall from your own steadfastness.* [27] Dad, am I the *"unlearned and unstable"* man, *"wresting"* the Sacred Scripture to my own destruction? There are things in the Bible hard to understand! Will I claim that Drew Emmans can understand these *"hard to understand"* passages? Or do I rather, as a youth pastor, lead my kids to fall because they themselves were led aside by the *"error of the unwise?"* And how will I know for sure, one way or the other? I will say again, the fear of God lay heavy on my soul.

Some people said at the time that this is all too complicated, and that I am "over-intellectualizing" things, that its "all about a relationship with Jesus, not some complicated theology," and "where's your faith, Drew?" God wouldn't make things so difficult, they told me. I heard these claims then, and I heard the same things when I left the *Novus Ordo*, Vatican II sect (which is, ultimately, just another Protestant sect). But what kind of "relationship" do I have with our Blessed Lord and Savior Jesus Christ if I do not even take the time or care to learn what He commands, and then obey? We

---

[27] 2 Peter 3:16-18

owe to God right worship, and we *owe* to Him *all our obedience in every aspect and every moment of our lives.* Should I suppose that Christ does not mind if I tell my high school kids something false about His sacred Person, and what He requires for worship and obedience, as long as my "heart is in the right place?" Does God take pleasure in fools?[28] We are even told to pluck out an offending eye to avoid hell, but I am being overly concerned with these things?[29] And as to the oft-repeated suggestion to just "have faith," I have to point out that the nature of faith is precisely one of the issues at stake! Unless, of course, faith just means an act of the will whereby I convince myself not to worry about anything, because it is all about the "relationship..."

Thus, I began to realize and articulate what was at stake. There was no ultimate authority for defining the parameters of faith and of the Bible, and each man was his own Pope. Indeed, each man literally *invented* his own Christianity, authoritatively promulgated his own laws and dogmas, and each man hurled anathemas at any who dared question his "exegesis" of the Bible. I realized that there was no way for anyone to say *with any authority beyond his own opinion* that BP's church of chaos was radically disordered

---

[28] Ecclesiastes 5:4
[29] Mathew 18:9

and false. BP is just like Pastor Cedric, who is just like Martin Luther, who in turn is just like Drew Emmans. We all just create our little mini-faiths and mini-churches, based on our own infallible authority, and our own interpretation of a vernacular translation of the Bible, and picking and choosing amongst the legion of existent theologies and theologians. We never admit it, of course, saying rather that we base everything on the Word of God, and maybe combined with a hypocritical appeal to some theological tradition ("Calvin says X," that kind of thing). That is, I think, more than not admitting it, *we just don't see it.* But we ultimately oppose our interpretation of the Bible to everyone else's interpretation, and that against the various reformers; and all of these against the Catholic Church's interpretation!

The horror with which this filled me is hard to put into words. Dad, I want the truth! I am not smart enough to create anew my own brand of Christianity, and even if I were smart enough, I would still flee from such a task. Where is the "pillar?"[30] Where is the "city set on the hill?"[31] To whom do I go to receive the words of eternal life?[32] No, I want the true faith that has been "handed down!" Received, not made!

---

[30] 1 Timothy 3:15
[31] Mathew 5:14
[32] 6:68

Received, even if it looked far different than what I was used to, and even if it meant great suffering and personal cost to receive it. I was not content to wander the vast wasteland of various *probable opinions* about God and salvation. Too much hung in the balance. I refused then and I refuse now to lose the Pearl of Great Price because I trusted my own powers of Biblical exegesis, or because I liked the sound of Pastor Cedric's theology, for instance.

So, even as the shadows lengthened, I did not abandon hope. No, I believed then, just as I believe now, *that Christianity is true, absolutely true, because our Blessed Lord and Savior Jesus Christ is the Truth.* So, I said to myself, there has to be a way out. There has to be a way to square this circle. I couldn't see how it could be possible, but I knew it *must* be possible. I spent some months in this terrible state, searching for the way out that I knew must exist.

I don't know if I have ever told you about the moment when I found the answer. Or rather, I didn't find it; it was given to me. Perhaps it will sound as though I am overstating things, maybe for dramatic effect, but there it is. I will attempt to describe it, in all honesty, and you can do with it what you will.

I had been severely depressed and in a state of utmost confusion, as I have said, since I had attended the youth pastor retreat in L.A. On this particular morning, I was driving to William Jessup University as usual, in my truck. As usual, my mind was going around and around, trying to find a way out of what I had long since realized was a matter of *first principles*, not one of a particular interpretation of some verse in the Bible. There was a flaw somewhere in my first principles, the very premises upon which everything else relied, but I could not locate it. As I drove, hunched over the wheel, depressed and disturbed, turning everything I had so far learned over and over again in my head, a thought came suddenly to my mind.

I don't say I actively thought of it; it came to me. It was of a memory of something that I had heard once, years before maybe on the radio, that there actually *was* a church that claimed for itself *the absolute authority to interpret the Bible*, and one that backed that claim by a further claim to trace its beginnings and authority not to some church split, or to the Reformers, but even to Christ Himself. The Catholic Church claimed for itself the prerogative to infallibly interpret the Bible, and to command the will in the name of Christ, obligating belief. This was no more than a bit of useless trivia that I thought an absurd and pointless claim at the time that I heard it, just something any strange non-Christian group might say. I had heard some various things about the Catholic Church over the years, of course, but this particular claim I had only heard in passing, and I don't know that I had ever thought of it again, beyond that one time I heard it. But the memory was there, locked far away with a billion other useless facts, and at that moment it came from nowhere with unbelievable force and clarity: the Catholic Church!

I don't want to claim for myself an experience like that of Saint Paul's, but I really did almost have to pull the truck over along highway 65. I was flooded by that feeling of joyful exhilaration comingled with sheer terror that one sometimes gets when on a rollercoaster let's say, or upon receiving the most wonderful news that a child will soon be born. I saw, in an instant, the only way out. Of course! It all fits! There *has* to be such an authoritative body, *or all Christianity is nothing more than a big "church of chaos!"*

I was shaking when I pulled up to WJU, and my mind was racing. It was as clear as day, and I knew at that very moment that this was the only way out. "But wait," I told myself, "Slow down! Catholics worship Mary, they worship statues, and *they are not even Christians*! What about the Crusades and the Inquisition? This cannot be the way out!

Slow down!" I thought about this all day, paying absolutely no attention to my classes. "But what do I actually know about Catholics?" I finally asked myself. "I have heard all these terrible things about them, even that the Pope is the antichrist, but what do I really *know*?" By the way, I didn't even really know at the time what or who the Pope was. "I know what the media, PBS, The New York Times, and everyone else says about Evangelical Christians, and I know that most of it is absolutely false. It is slanderous and calumnious, and I know, because I am one. So, maybe it is the same way with the Catholics. I would want someone who is looking into what Evangelicals believe to go directly to the Evangelical sources, and not to the manifest enemies of Evangelicalism. If I want to know what it actually is that Catholics believe, it would be unjust to merely trust the word of those who hate the Catholic Church. So, I will endeavor to find out *what the Catholic Church says about herself.* And I will reserve judgment about the 'Road to Damascus' experience I just had. I will not give intellectual assent until and unless I am sure."

Thus, I began a year and a half of study. First, I went to Borders and Barnes & Nobles, to the "Christianity" section. I literally knew almost nothing about the Church, so I began to read books in the "Catholicism 101" genre. When I had depleted the big bookstores' reserves in this area, I began to secretly haunt the Catholic bookstores in Roseville and Sacramento. I began to read histories of the Protestant Reformation, and of the Catholic Church. It was laborious and disturbing. I felt as though I was plunging into the rabbit hole, from which there could be no return to normalcy. The excitement I had felt when I first thought that this might be the only way out was replaced by the deep and ominous dread *that this might, indeed, be the only way out.* I began to see what was at stake, and what it would cost if I continued to follow the truth.

The Castle

There is so much to say about that year and a half. It was one of agony and ecstasy, of the thrill of discovery, and of the pursuit of truth, and also of sheer terror at the prospect of giving intellectual assent to what was, more and more, becoming manifest.

I will touch briefly upon some of the things that I discovered over the course of that time: first, I began to realize that there was far more to the Christian faith than I had ever before realized. It was a feeling of having spent one's life in the antechamber of a great palace, never setting foot inside the glorious and magnificent City of God, but remaining only in the foyer, foolishly thinking the foyer was all there was. There were treasures found inside the castle that the foyer could but merely hint at, and give but a pale reflection.[33] And I quickly realized that those things that were, for me, non-

---

[33] I think I may have borrowed this analogy from the writer of vampire stories, Anne Rice. She converted to *Novus Ordo* Catholicism in 1998, and then publicly abandoned the religion twelve years later. It may have been an essay she wrote about her conversion that included something like the above image; or perhaps it was borrowed from somewhere else. Whatever the case, it is not mine, but resonates very deeply with my own experience.

negotiable so to speak, were found in all their splendor in the Catholic Church. But they were transformed from something small and thin, to something indescribably great, infinite and profound. I have previously mentioned the feeling I had, as a boy, that our Protestant Christianity had a strange "thinness" to it, if you recall. Upon discovering the Catholic Church, this feeling was exploded and laid to rest for good. There was a history to Christianity that was wide, deep, and glorious.

And Jesus Christ was still the Incarnate Word, fully God and fully man, formed in the immaculate womb of the Blessed Virgin Mary. There was no diminution or dissolution of His Sacred Person. On the contrary, Christ took on the aspect also of the great King of the Universe, whose reign was not limited to some "invisible church," but rather extended to every single individual aspect of creation without distinction. Christ is the sovereign King, and He exercises also a *Social Kingship* over all human activity. "Freedom of religion" is a demonic freedom, an antichrist freedom. No one has a "right" to worship false gods. We are not free to do evil, but rather made free to choose the good. All persons and all nations are obligated to submit without reservation to the King of Kings and Lord of Lords.

The Person of our Blessed Lord and Savior Jesus Christ was by no means diminished, and the history of the Church was vast and glorious. Christianity was so much larger in this respect also: in the Sacraments. The Mass, I learned, is the means by which the one sacrifice of our Blessed Lord and Savior is perpetuated through time, and the means by which even Drew Emmans can "eat his flesh and drink his blood," and so have divine Life within.[34] It is the sacred prayer of the Church, guarded jealously in all its integrity these two thousand years, and is still the ultimate source of all grace in the world. It is the "perpetual sacrifice," the one and the same sacrifice on Calvary, made present on all the Catholic altars throughout the world, wherever Mass is said. It is the reason that all over Christendom monuments have been raised to the honor of His sacred Person, those greatest of human architectural triumphs, the Cathedrals and churches. There is found nothing like them in all the world, and they exist solely to be temples of the Living God, where the second Person of the Ever Blessed Trinity comes to dwell with man. *"Et Verbum caro factum est, et habitavit in nobis."*[35] These sometimes massive, sometimes small, beautiful, and intimate monuments to the Christian faith were built as a fitting place

---

[34] John 6:56
[35] John 1:14, "And the Word was made flesh and dwelt among us."

in which to immolate the supreme sacrifice, and to house the Sacred Species, now, by the power of the Holy Spirit, made the very Flesh and Blood of Christ. (The difference between a Catholic Church building and a Protestant church building is absolutely striking. The places of worship with which I was acquainted, the Protestant churches, were actually barren, empty, ugly, and often were literally warehouses). And inside each magnificent Catholic Church, on each altar of carven and ornate stone, is a small box, adorned in gold and precious stones. Inside each of these tabernacles is the body and blood of our Blessed Lord, sacramentally present for our worship and consumption. Chesterton has poetically described the Tabernacle thus:

> "The hidden room in a man's house
> Where God sits all the year,
> The secret window whence the world
> Looks small and very dear."[36]

But if I found the history of the Catholic Church to be astonishing and wonderful, I was filled with absolute dread when I found out what all Christians had unanimously believed concerning the moral life. It was far removed from

---

[36] Chesterton, G.K. *Lepanto*, Ignatius Press, 2004, Dale Ahlquist, Editor. Pg. 16, pp. 110.

the life we lived as evangelical Protestants. I will mention one sin in particular, at once heinous and ubiquitous, because it illustrates precisely the end result of listening to heretics.

I hope that what I say next is not construed as a merely a vulgar discussion of the intimacy and mystery of the marital act. The world is so vile and wicked in this regard, that it makes so free to speak openly and perversely about what should be guarded reverently, where even angels fear to tread. The profanation of all things sacred has reached such a point of saturation that modesty in speech and dress is no longer a virtue, but even has become for this wicked world a vice. Let what follows be received with this in mind.

Dan K. was the only person I considered to be something of a "spiritual authority" who spoke to me before my marriage about birth control. He said, perhaps surprisingly, that birth control should not be used. It was the first and only time I had heard of birth control one way or the other, in the context of Christian marriage. But Dan also told me (possibly the same day) that he thought that polygamy was just fine, as long as the civil authorities had not banned it! The only reason that I can't have several wives, according to Dan's interpretation of the Bible, is because it is against the laws of the state in which we happen to live; another example of the

77

insanity of *sola scriptura*. Because I found this preposterous, I did not really take what he said about birth control too seriously.

Thus, when we were married, no one told us that our publicly broadcasted "five-year plan," by which we meant that we would intentionally frustrate the marital act so as to not have children for five years, was morally despicable. It was utterly depraved, and would have earned us the just censure by our friends and family in a different age. But this is a dark and wicked age, so no one warned us that birth control had been condemned universally, not only by the One True Church, but even by all, or at least the vast majority, of the Protestant sects. No one told me the history of the "pill," and how it is inextricably linked to abortion and the public acclamation of sodomy. No one warned me that the acceptance of birth control had only crept even into the Protestant sects in something like the 1920's or '30's, through one of the Anglican sect's "conferences."[37] No one warned me that it is connected directly with the onslaught of divorce, and the destruction of the family. No one told me that it would both kill my soul and maybe snuff out the lives of my unborn children. Did you know that the popular "pill" that is regularly

---

[37] Lambeth Conference, 1930. Resolution 15.

sold to women (and children) sometimes acts as an abortifacient? Dad, because I did not know this, there is a chance that one or more of your grandchildren have been killed in the womb. Why didn't you warn me about this danger, this danger to my soul, my children, and my marriage? Is it because you didn't know? But how could you not know something that impinges so directly on human life and death, on the sixth commandment, on the inviolable nature of the family, on the salvation of souls, on foundation of human society, and on the furthering and building up of the Kingdom of God? Did your 30-year study of the Bible not throw any light onto this? How could you not know something that has been spoken about, defined, and clarified many, many times in the history of the Church? I ask all this rhetorically.

And even when a chemical that can cause abortions is not used, birth control is still fatal to the soul, and destructive to marriages and civilization. It inverts the ends of marriage, making pleasure the principal end, and fecundity subordinate to pleasure, or to some other end. But if the principal end of the marital act is pleasure, then what is the principal end of marriage itself? It can only be pleasure. But this is not so in a Christian marriage, regardless of what the pagans are doing. In a true Christian marriage pleasure, the help and support of the spouses, companionship, etc., are all real and valuable ends, but they are all absolutely subordinate to procreation and the Christian education of children. If they are not subordinated, then on what basis can you argue that marriages cannot be broken on the basis of feelings, or a "failure of love," or any reason whatsoever? How can you argue that marriage is the only context in which the marital act can be performed? Indeed, why is it, do you suppose, that the so-called "marriage" of sexual deviants is now sweeping the entire world? The entire "sexual revolution" that is now destroying the last vestiges of Christian civilization is premised on the widespread use and acceptance of birth control. This widespread use and acceptance are premised upon the inversion of the ends in marriage. And it was the Protestants who sold out *en masse* to this zeitgeist from hell.

Further, how many Evangelical Christian men do you know who have surgically sterilized themselves, or had their wives surgically sterilized, so as to avoid once and for all the possibility of fecundity in the marital act? I know many. Is this a positive good, or a grave evil? It can only be one or the other. And if you say it is evil, on what basis can you possibly say it? The principle is the same as that of any other kind of contraception. Fecundity is subordinated to pleasure, or financial considerations, or convenience, or whatever. It doesn't matter at that point. If you say that it is a positive good, then the principle has been irrevocably ceded. Once you cede the principle, then Margret Sanger wins. And she has definitely won. Christendom has been contracepted, aborted, sterilized, and sodomized out of existence. *"A voice was heard in Rama, weeping and great mourning, Rachel weeping for her children; and she refused to be comforted, because they were no more."*[38]

I will also mention, because it is relevant to this present consideration, that during my time at William Jessup University, when I was just discovering the chaos of Protestantism but before I had been given the way out, I had an illuminating conversation with a fellow student. This young lady was the daughter of a pastor; she was a self-professed Evangelical Christian, and student in good standing at an Evangelical Christian University; and she was proudly pro-abortion. Not only this, but also her entire church was pro-abortion, led by her father the pastor. Now, Dad, you can argue that this is an aberration, and that obviously no one can be pro-abortion and an Evangelical Christian at the same time. But on what basis do you make that claim? Point me to the authoritative body that can say, in an exercise of Divine

---

[38] Jeremiah 31:15

authority that has the power to command the will, that this is impossible. Dad says it is so. But is Dad infallible? You say it is obviously the teaching of the Bible. I answer that the Pastor in question also reads his Bible, perhaps as much or even more than does Dad. Further, where in the Bible is abortion univocally mentioned, let alone condemned? I fear that it is not mentioned at all. So, you might want to claim that this "shepherd of souls" is a false shepherd, and you will be right, but what principled reason can you give to make that claim? What rationale can you provide that is compatible with your Protestant premises? You will say it is against the Ten Commandments. It surely is, but I thought the Ten Commandments do not bind a Christian? If say this is false, and they certainly do bind a Christian, then I say it is your opinion against Dr. Piper's and Martin Luther's, to name just two. Will you point me to the unanimous tradition of the various Protestant sects, and even that of the Catholic Church, perhaps? To this several responses can be given. First, it is manifestly not the unanimous tradition of the Protestant sects, even if it is a majority tradition. Second, you reject *my* appeal to tradition concerning birth control in general, and the Catholic Church in particular. You reject it as the "tradition of men!" So, why could not this young lady reject your chauvinist "tradition of men" relating to the "right of a woman to control her own fertility?" No, you will forgive me if I do not find this appeal to tradition very convincing. *Any* appeal to tradition is explicitly rejected in the very founding principles of your religion.

I do not bring all this up to try to make you feel guilty, or to insinuate that you are complicit in murder. I do not know for sure whether our use of this evil resulted in the death of one of our children, but I don't think that it did. We did not use the "Pill" for long, because Jamiey soon learned that it might kill our children, but we continued to use various other means of birth control, to my eternal shame. We engaged, unwittingly, in this wickedness until I stumbled onto the fact that it had been universally condemned, *even by the Protestant heretics*, until the twentieth century, and that it is a grave, *mortal* sin. We ceased using birth control at all once I discovered that fact, and we never looked back. Indeed, the whole thing is so shameful a memory to me that I hate even to think about it, let alone to publicize my sin in this way. I bring it up, rather, to illustrate why these considerations matter so much. The difference between the One True Church and all the legion counterfeits is by no means a matter of semantics, or the manipulation of Sacred Texts, but is rather the difference between heaven and hell. Our souls really do hang in the balance, Satan is really our enemy, and he is really a *liar*. Satan and his wolves will ravage any fool who leaves the one flock of Christ, and drag his soul to hell. It is a necessary law of our fallen nature, and of our fallen world. From the beginning Satan has hated women and children, and thus has hated families. He hates them because he hates the Blessed Virgin Mary, and he hates her because he hates her Divine Son. And because he hates the Holy Family, he also hates my wife and my children. I will not leave my family to the ravages of the wolves, in the person of false shepherds and counterfeit sects. No, I will rather flee to the only place of refuge and safety: the Holy, Roman Catholic Church.

So, I had realized that the history of Christianity is deep and wide, and that the moral and spiritual life of normal Christians throughout the ages is radically different from the Evangelical life I had heretofore lived. The rupture was so profound, that I immediately realized the implication. *I was in a state of mortal sin so great that I would be justly and immediately sent to hell for my sins, if I were to die.* But it is enough to read the Bible without the blinders imposed by the original Protestant heretics to see that this is so. The Bible unequivocally demands obedience to the commandments of Christ, and to the Ten Commandments, and does so over and over again. Further, the Bible warns over and over again to avoid the death-dealing tongues of the heretics. Why on earth,

I asked myself, would I stake my soul on the mass of chaos and disorder that is the Protestant world, and on the teachings of Father Martin Luther, the apostate monk? Why would I do it? Why not join the Manicheans, or the Nestorians, or the Arians, or the Greek Orthodox, etc., etc., *ad infinitum*? Do I care so little for my soul that I would follow blindly any one of these various groups, which you yourself admit are heretics? Indeed, do I care so little about the texts of the Bible that I do not tremble when I see them manipulated, abused, perverted, and maliciously interpreted? No, to stay in the antechamber is madness, and to stay on a branch that is even now withering on the ground is madness. I had to seek the vine from which these various branches have so decisively detached themselves, and to enter that great Castle, to which our love for Jesus Christ must necessarily lead, if we really do love Him as we claim.

There was a certain strangeness to all this, because I was at first worried that Catholicism was so unlike what I had been led to believe constituted Christianity. Now, the basics were there, as I have said. Jesus is really God and really man, and the Bible is really the inspired, inerrant Word of God. These I had always believed since my youth, and I had believed rightly. But so much else was strange. The Sacraments, the Mass, the statues, the Saints, the Blessed

Virgin Mary, these were all utterly foreign. Indeed, as with most Protestants, I had so imbibed the poison of the heretics that I had come almost to *hate* the Blessed Virgin, the very Mother of God. I didn't hate her in a conscious way, of course, and I would have even said that I called her "Blessed," as she herself had prophesied that "all generations" would.[39] But I never did actually call her that, and I never actually thought about her at all. Not an active hate, necessarily, but the pagans and the atheists, and the various practitioners of false religions might not actively and consciously hate Jesus Christ either, but it is hate nonetheless. Indifference to the truth and hatred of the truth go hand in hand.

In this regard, I think it would be helpful to say a few words, because this really affected me at the time. I said to myself then, "But Drew, if you were an atheist, or an agnostic, or whatever, and you had never heard the claims of the Faith, how would you respond? That is to say, if a Protestant of some sort approached you, and told you about the Protestant faith, what would be your response? You would think it the strangest thing in the world to believe that a *virgin could become pregnant with her Maker, and that the infinite God, the second Person of the Blessed Trinity, could become*

---

[39] Luke 1:48

incarnate in the womb of a virgin. Strange does not even begin to describe it! But I, Drew Emmans, have no problem believing that a virgin conceived, and that God became man. So why do I think that it is a bridge too far that this same Virgin was prepared by her own immaculate conception, which was itself an utterly gratuitous gift of God, to be the mother of our savior? Why would I find it surprising that our Blessed Savior protected His own Blessed Mother from the ravages of Satan in the form of original or personal sin? Why can I assert with a straight face that she was a virgin when she conceived, but then I bizarrely say that she could not have possibly remained a virgin, because, well, that would be crazy?"

I realized at the time the insanity of such a position; and, I also realized then, much of it is because we Protestants don't really believe in the Incarnation at all. We assert a kind of belief, of course, but we can't really believe it, or we would be utterly struck by the profundity of the role of the Blessed Virgin Mary. *"And whence is this to me, that the mother of my Lord should come to me?"*[40] We say that the Virgin was the spouse of the Holy Spirit who overshadowed her so that she conceived. And then we simultaneously assert, without a

---

[40] Luke 1:43

hint of shame, that she also had merely human children by Joseph. My whole being revolts at even writing these blasphemous words! No, if we really believed in the Incarnation, we couldn't possibly believe that she also bore merely human children. I had to grapple with this realization over ten years ago, and it came to me then that the problem was in me. *I was a blasphemer, a man of little faith, a heretic of the worst kind, and a credulous fool who believed anything any other heretic might tell him, but who impiously refused to believe what the True Church herself proposed for belief!*

Dad, you taught me throughout my childhood to keep the faith, so that I can go to heaven and there forever behold the One for whom and by whom all the cosmos was created. I believed you then, and I believe you now. I strove to keep the faith then, as I do now. But if I ask, "What *is* the faith?" how will you reply? You will say, "read the Bible." But Dad, I am the Ethiopian Eunuch, to whom the Apostle Phillip said, "*Thinkest thou that thou understandest what thou readest?*"[41] I answer with the Ethiopian: "*How can I, unless some man show me?*" Further, as I have said repeatedly, there are things in Sacred Scripture that are "*hard to understand!*" No, I am

[41] Acts 8:31 This may have been Philip the Deacon, and not the Evangelist. The point stands, however; he is a formal representative of the hierarchy of the Catholic Church.

neither smart enough nor wise enough to interpret the Sacred Texts; I need "*some man to show me.*" And when I looked further into this problem, I found that the faith *includes* Sacred Scripture, but is by no means coterminous with it. Again, this should be obvious, because even our devotion to the Sacred Texts is predicated on actually having a reliable copy of the correct texts, in a translation that is true to the original languages, and having been taught that what is contained in the Texts is really the inerrant Word of God, and not just another ancient manuscript, or something like the Koran or Book or Mormon, or whatever. But the words of the Bible were really written in ink, by real flesh and blood humans, who were really otherwise prone to err and sin, even as we are. So how do you know that the Bible is infallible? Why do you say that the Bible has been protected and inspired by the power of the Holy Spirit against the weakness of the frail instruments who actually wrote it, but then impiously maintain that the same Holy Spirit is incapable of likewise protecting and guiding the Church in her laws, Sacraments, liturgies, doctrines and dogmas throughout the entire life of the Church in her militant state? And this *precisely so ignorant and sinful people like Drew Emmans can know exactly what we must believe and do in order to be saved?*

Thus it was that I came to the principle upon which everything else in the Christian faith is predicated; it is the principle of Divine authority. Everything that I had heretofore believed I believed because my father had taught me; I believed because my father and my mother believed; it had been handed down to me, received, not made; so I thought. And I thought that what my parents had received was simply the One True Faith, handed down from Christ to the Apostles, from the Apostles through the Church and the Bible, and that to me. But everything I had discovered during those two years falsified this simplistic understanding, and everything had led to this crisis of authority. What was needed, indeed what was absolutely necessary, was an authority that is not merely human, not merely capable of learning Greek and teaching about the Bible, for instance, not *merely* a teaching power at all, but a power that wielded *Divine* authority to teach and to *command*. What was necessary was a power to "bind and to loose" in the name of God.[42] From what source could such a power derive? There is only one God, so there can be only one source. Christ Himself has that power, a power He received from His

---

[42] Mathew 18:18

Father: *"He was teaching them as one having authority, and not as their scribes."*[43]

What I learned during those years was precisely that this Divine Voice still speaks, and has spoken for 2,000 years. Christ did indeed give His own authority to His Apostles, and they in turn gave it their successors. Saint Peter, the one for whom our Lord prayed that *his faith would not fail*, was given the primacy of that authority, as the very vicar of Christ on earth. The Church is really a Kingdom, and is really a monarchy, with Christ as the King, and the Pope as His Vicar. We ourselves are mere sheep!

Christ is not among us visibly, but only sacramentally and in the person of His Vicar. But His delegated authority as King of Kings and Lord of Lords He entrusted to His Church, *"the pillar and foundation of the truth."* And the Church can only be the pillar and foundation of the truth if it is protected from error by the power of the Holy Spirit, and if it can bind and loose *both on earth and in heaven.* Thus, it was with the authority of Christ through His Church that the Bible was composed, protected, translated, interpreted, promulgated and disseminated throughout the world. It was with the authority of Christ Himself that the faith was defined

---

[43] Mathew 7:29. See also: Mathew 28:18; Mathew 16:13-19.

and defended in Councils and in Creeds. Saint Paul himself wielded this authority when he hurled his anathemas, and the Church wielded it when she pronounced proscribed and condemned all the perversity of the heretics. Christ Himself anathematized Arius and Nestorius, through His Church and through His Vicar, and it was Christ Himself who anathematized the wicked heresies of Luther and Calvin at Trent. Indeed, the only way that the Bible can be true and trustworthy is if that Divine authority, breathed so long ago onto the Apostles, is still able to speak, to teach, to command, to condemn and to forgive. Everything hangs on this Divine Authority.[44]

So it was that I came to believe. I assented to everything that God had revealed, for the sole motive that God had revealed it, "God who can neither deceive nor be deceived." I often describe the experience thus: with fear and trembling I stumbled at the age of 26, as one untimely born, across the threshold of the Catholic Church.

---

[44] I think that much of the ideas and phrasing of this paragraph, as well as others in this letter, is probably borrowed, at least in spirit, from Cardinal Manning's wonderful little book: The Grounds of Faith. Four Lectures.

The New Beginning

It seems to me, when I examine all my 36-year history, a history that is nothing less than another example of God's unspeakable condescension and love, that I am in many ways like a literary figure that we both know and love, Lucy Pevensies. (It seems that I often can be compared to those figures that seem at first glance to be quite inapposite; for instance, I hope that it goes without saying that I am probably unlike the Ethiopian Eunuch in every possible way except a weak analogy of faith!). Lucy sees Aslan at night, if you remember the scene in Prince Caspian, from a distance, and she realizes that Aslan is asking her to follow him.[45] She immediately goes and wakens her siblings, and tells them that she has seen Aslan. But they do not believe her, and so, in tears, she stays with her siblings. Later in the story they meet Aslan again after a series of disasters, and Lucy excitedly tells Aslan that she had seen him that night, and that she had told her siblings, but they wouldn't

[45] Lewis, C.S. *Prince Caspian.* Scholastic, 1995.

believe her. But Aslan is not pleased with her for this. He asks her, or intimates the question, "Why did you yourself not follow?" Lucy is surprised and devastated, if you can recall the scene. She didn't really think that she could follow without the rest of her family. She was nobody, the smallest of her family, the least likely to head off on her own in a strange land, following Aslan through the night. In an analogous way, I am the least of the Emmans men in every respect. I am the least talented, the least intelligent, the least wise, and the one with the weakest faith. But Dad, what can I do when, despite my utter inadequacies, I too have seen Aslan?

I promised our Lord that I would obey Him and follow Him, no matter where He led, and no matter what the cost. Christ has shown Himself to me in His Church. I excitedly told my family, just like Lucy, and my family would not believe me, at least not all of them, and at least not at first. And my father still refuses to believe. Very well. We are all answerable ultimately to God alone. But *I* must obey. Woe to me, Dad, if I do not obey. Shall I take lightly the mercy and grace of God? Shall I despise His guidance and His voice? Dad, if you had not prayed for me, and if you yourself had not shown me what it was to follow hard after God, I might have rebelled against you in my youth. If I had rebelled against you in my youth, I might have long since apostatized completely. If I had apostatized, I would have never met and married my beautiful wife, who is practically perfect in every way, and who in turn saved me from sliding into indifference and complete spiritual death. If I had not repented for my sin during my mishandling of our family affairs, and if I had not then promised God that I would obey Him no matter what the cost, I would have never become a youth pastor. If I had never become a youth pastor, I most likely would have never seen the impossibility and contradiction of the Protestant heresy. If I had not seen this, I would have never entered what I had erroneously considered to be the Catholic Church. If I had not entered the *Novus Ordo*, Vatican II church, I would never have moved my family to Ave Maria, a decision that was, prescinding from decisions directly related to the faith, the second-best decision I have ever made in my life (marrying my wife was the best without qualification). If we had not moved to Ave, I would have never discovered that the church of Vatican II is the church of the antichrist, the ape of the One True Church, the almost certain forerunner of the ultimate Antichrist, and the diabolical vehicle that has brought the "abomination of desolation" and the almost complete cessation of the Eternal Sacrifice. If I had not done all this I would not now be counted among the surviving remnant of the Catholic Church. All this I have because Christ has been so merciful to me, and because I have been given the grace to obey. Shall I now despise His grace?

Indeed, Dad, it should be clear from all this that you really have no one but yourself to blame for our conversion to the Catholic Church. The entire blame (or all the praise!) can be laid completely at your feet. You told us that Jesus is the Truth, and we believed you. You told us to follow the Truth wherever He may lead, and we believed you. You told us that God really does answer prayers, and we believed you. And you, yourself, prayed for us from the earliest moments of our existence, and God heard your prayers.

Thus, through all of this, as I have often wondered why it is that God has been so merciful to me and my family, and brought us so far, I realize that there are, ultimately, two proximate, efficient causes. The first and most important *is your and Mom's faithfulness to the light that you had*, and your constant prayers on our behalf. The other is my agonized prayer, early in life, that God is even now in the process of answering. My early prayer was itself a gift of God, brought about by your intercession on my behalf. Both these proximate causes are nothing but the movement of pure grace, and the graced movement of our own wills to respond. You and Mom are brands plucked from the fire; do you now think that God will not hear your prayers, when you have begged Him these last 36 years of my life that I will be saved? Do you think that God's hand is so short that cannot likewise rescue your other sons and your daughter, your daughters-in-law, your son-in-law, and your grandchildren, from the final death?

We were not there 2,000 years ago to receive the revelation. It was not our eyes that beheld the Incarnate Word ascend in to heaven, nor our ears that heard him teach during those three years of public ministry, nor our hands that touched His Sacred Person, the Lamb of God whose blood is shed for the world's sins. The only way we know anything about it at all is because Christ founded a Church, and gave His own authority to the Apostles, along with the mission to "go into all the world." That mission continues even in these dark and probably final days, and has even now arrived at our own doorstep. Christ knocks at the door of our souls even now, in the person of His Body, the Church. So, if I want to assert that the Bible is the infallible word of God, I can only do so based on the same infallible authority that has promulgated, protected, defined, and interpreted the Sacred Texts for these two thousand years. And anything less would not be supernatural faith, "but only a sort of faith in my own opinion."[46]

Dad, the whole thing rises and falls on the same Divine authority. The Catholic faith does not hang on any particular distorted interpretation that can be given to an ancient text penned by a Church Father, nor any particular spin a heretic might put onto Sacred Scripture, but rather depends solely on the Divine authority given by Christ to the Apostles and to their successors. This, I think, is the main thing that I wanted to communicate to you with this letter. There are no salacious tidbits of history, or selected quotations from Saint Augustine or the Fathers, or some "hard to understand" verse of the Bible that can be twisted or interpreted to mean that the Catholic Church is not the One True Church. No, the whole edifice, Church and Bible, is predicated on God revealing, and God "can neither deceive nor be deceived." There is then, as I realized all those ten years ago, one of two options available to us: *tertium non est datur.*[47] Either the Catholic Church is precisely who she claims to be, or none of it can possibly be true, not Jesus, not the Bible, none of it. We either give intellectual assent to *everything* that has been revealed, *because God has revealed*

---

[46] ST II-II, q. 5, a. 3, *Respondeo.*
[47] "A third [option] is not given."

it, or admit that everything is chaos and the void, and the whole world is a cosmic accident.

But, Dad, the whole world *is not* a cosmic accident. Therefore...

The End

I will conclude this overly long *apologia pro vita sua* here. I don't know whether this letter will help you understand why I can never leave the Church, and I suspect, given my oft-noted inability to give intelligible form to my convictions, that there is still much that will remain opaque. This cannot be helped, I suppose, and is a consequence of my being a fallen human being. But I do hope you take this letter in the spirit in which it was offered. It is an attempt to clarify why exactly I entered the Catholic Church in the first place, and why it is impossible that I could ever leave it. The deluge is coming, both in the wicked and decaying world at large, and in our own rapidly approaching personal judgment, when we will stand before the sovereign Judge of every soul, to give an account of everything we have said, thought, and done. When that deluge hits, and it will certainly hit, I want to be found nowhere but in the sole Ark of Salvation, the One, Holy, Roman, Catholic and Apostolic Church. If I be found anywhere else at that moment, I fear that I shall certainly perish in the flood.

Your affectionate and loyal son,

Drew

Lucca, Italy
February 5th
The Feast of Saint Agatha, *Anno Domini,* 2016

P.S. I know that the verbosity of my correspondence is off-putting. Nevertheless, I am going to make so bold as to ask you to read a further treatise, as a favor to me, if you can find the time. It is the best concise treatment of this same topic that I have yet come across, and is both accessible and succinct. It is: <u>The Grounds of Faith: Four Lectures</u>. By Henry Edward Cardinal Manning.

Andrew Emmans lives in Washington State with his family.

He can be reached at: drewemmans@gmail.com